FREEDOM AND PUBLIC FAITH.

SPEECH

OF

WILLIAM H. SEWARD,

ON THE

ABROGATION OF THE MISSOURI COMPROMISE,

IN THE

KANSAS AND NEBRASKA BILLS.

SENATE OF THE UNITED STATES, FEBRUARY 17, 1854.

WASHINGTON, D. C.
BUELL & BLANCHARD, PRINTERS.
1854.

SPEECH OF WILLIAM H. SEWARD.

MR. PRESIDENT:

The United States, at the close of the Revolution, rested southward on the St. Mary's, and westward on the Mississippi, and possessed a broad, unoccupied domain, circumscribed by those rivers, the Alleghany mountains, and the great Northern lakes. The Constitution anticipated the division of this domain into States, to be admitted as members of the Union, but it neither provided for nor anticipated any enlargement of the national boundaries. The People, engaged in reorganizing their Governments, improving their social systems, and establishing relations of commerce and friendship with other nations, remained many years content within their apparently ample limits. But it was already foreseen that the free navigation of the Mississippi would soon become an urgent public want.

France, although she had lost Canada, in chivalrous battle, on the Heights of Abraham, in 1763, nevertheless, still retained her ancient territories on the western bank of the Mississippi. She had also, just before the breaking out of her own fearful revolution, re-acquired, by a secret treaty, the possessions on the Gulf of Mexico, which, in a recent war, had been wrested from her by Spain. Her First Consul, among those brilliant achievements which proved him the first Statesman as well as the first Captain of Europe, sagaciously sold the whole of these possessions to the United States, for a liberal sum, and thus replenished his treasury, while he saved from his enemies, and transferred to a friendly Power, distant and vast regions, which, for want of adequate naval force, he was unable to defend.

This purchase of Louisiana from France, by the United States, involved a grave dispute concerning the western limits of that province; and that controversy, having remained open until 1819, was then adjusted by a treaty, in which they relinquished Texas to Spain, and accepted a cession of the early-discovered and long-inhabited provinces of East Florida and West Florida. The United States stipulated, in each of these cases, to admit the countries thus annexed into the Federal Union.

The acquisitions of Oregon, by discovery and occupation, of Texas, by her voluntary annexation, and of New Mexico and California, including what is now called Utah, by war, completed that rapid course of enlargement, at the close of which our frontier has been fixed near the centre of what was New Spain, on the Atlantic side of the continent, while on the west, as on the east, only an ocean separates us from the nations of the old world. It is not in my way now to speculate on the question, how long we are to rest on these advanced positions.

Slavery, before the Revolution, existed in all the thirteen Colonies, as it did also in nearly all the other European plantations in America. But it had been forced by British authority, for political and commercial ends, on the American People, against their own sagacious instincts of policy, and their stronger feelings of justice and humanity.

They had protested and remonstrated against the system, earnestly, for forty years, and they ceased to protest and remonstrate against it only when they finally committed their entire cause of complaint to the arbitrament of arms. An earnest spirit of emancipation was abroad in the Colonies at the close of the Revolution, and all of them, except, perhaps, South Carolina and Georgia, anticipated, desired, and designed an early removal of the system from the country. The suppression of the African slave trade, which was universally regarded as ancillary to that great measure, was not, without much reluctance, postponed until 1808.

While there was no national power, and no claim or desire for national power, anywhere, to compel involuntary emancipation in the States where slavery existed, there was at the same time a very general desire and a strong purpose to prevent its introduction into new communities yet to be formed, and into new States yet to be established. Mr. Jefferson proposed, as early as 1784, to exclude it from the national domain which should be constituted by cessions from the States to the United States. He recommended and urged the measure as ancillary, also, to the ultimate policy of emancipation. There seems to have been at first no very deep jealousy between the emancipating and the non-emancipating States; and the policy of admitting new States was not disturbed by questions concerning slavery. Vermont, a non-slaveholding State, was admitted in 1793. Kentucky, a tramontane slaveholding community, having been detached from Virginia, was admitted, without being questioned, about the same time. So, also, Tennessee, which was a similar community separated from North Carolina, was admitted in 1796, with a stipulation that the Ordinance which Mr. Jefferson had first proposed, and which had in the mean time been adopted for the Territory northwest of the Ohio, should not be held to apply within her limits. The same course was adopted in organizing Territorial Governments for Mississippi and Alabama, slaveholding communities which had been detached from South Carolina and Georgia. All these States and Territories were situated southwest of the Ohio river, all were more or less already peopled by slaveholders with their slaves; and to have excluded slavery within their limits would have been a national act, not of preventing the introduction of slavery, but of abolishing slavery. In short, the region southwest of the Ohio river presented a field in which the policy of preventing the introduction of slavery was impracticable. Our forefathers never attempted what was impracticable.

But the case was otherwise in that fair and broad region which stretched away from the banks of the Ohio, northward to the lakes, and westward to the Mississippi. It was yet free, or practically free, from the presence of slaves, and was nearly uninhabited, and quite unoccupied. There was then no Baltimore and Ohio railroad, no Erie railroad, no New York Central railroad, no Boston and Ogdensburgh railroad; there was no railroad through Canada; nor, indeed, any road around or across the mountains; no imperial Erie canal, no Welland canal, no lockages around the rapids and the falls of the St. Lawrence, the Mohawk, and the Niagara rivers, and no steam navigation on the lakes or on the Hudson, or on the Mississippi. There, in that remote and secluded region, the prevention of the introduction of slavery was possible; and there our forefathers, who left no possible national good unattempted, did prevent it. It makes one's heart bound with joy and gratitude, and lift itself up with mingled pride and veneration, to read the history of that great transaction. Discarding the trite and common forms of expressing the national will, they did not merely "vote," or "resolve," or "enact," as on other occasions, but they "ORDAINED," in language marked at once with precision, amplification, solemnity, and emphasis, that there "shall be neither slavery nor involuntary servitude in the said Territory, otherwise than in the punishment of crime, whereof the party shall have been duly convicted." And they further ORDAINED and declared that this law should be considered a COMPACT between the original States and the People and States of said Territory, and forever remain unalterable, unless by common consent. The Ordinance was agreed to unanimously. Virginia, in re-affirming her cession of the territory, ratified it, and the first Congress held under the Constitution solemnly renewed and confirmed it.

In pursuance of this Ordinance, the several Territorial Governments successively established in the Northwest Territory were organized with a prohibition of the introduction of slavery, and in due time, though at successive periods, Ohio, Indiana, Illinois, Michigan, and Wisconsin, States erected within that Territory, have come into the Union with Constitutions in their hands forever prohibiting slavery and involuntary servitude, except for the punishment of crime. They are yet young; but, nevertheless, who has ever seen elsewhere such States as they are! There are gathered the young, the vigorous, the active, the enlightened sons of every State, the flower and choice of every State in this broad Union; and there the emigrant for conscience sake, and for freedom's sake, from every land in Europe, from proud and all-conquering Britain, from heart-broken Ireland, from sunny Italy, from mercurial France, from spiritual Germany, from chivalrous Hungary, and from honest and brave old Sweden and Norway. Thence are already coming ample supplies of corn and wheat and wine for the manufacturers of the East, for the planters of the tropics, and even for the artisans and the armies of Europe; and thence will continue to come in long succession, as they have already begun to come, statesmen and legislators for this continent.

Thus it appears, Mr. President, that it was the policy of our fathers, in regard to the original domain of the United States, to prevent the introduction of slavery, wherever it was practicable. This policy encountered greater difficulites when it came under consideration with a view to its establishment in regions not included within our original domain. While slavery had been actually abolished already, by some of the emancipating States, several of them, owing to a great change in the relative value of the productions of slave labor, had fallen off into the class of non-emancipating States; and now the whole family of States was divided and classified as slaveholding or slave States, and non-slaveholding or free States. A rivalry for political ascendency was soon developed; and, besides the motives of interest and philanthropy which had before existed, there was now on each side a desire to increase, from among the candidates for admission into the Union, the number of States in their respective classes, and so their relative weight and influence in the Federal Councils.

The country which had been acquired from France was, in 1804, organized in two Territories, one of which, including New Orleans as its capital, was called Orleans, and the other, having St. Louis for its chief town, was called Louisiana. In 1812, the Territory of Orleans was admitted as a new State, under the name of Louisiana. It had been an old slaveholding colony of France, and the prevention of slavery within it would have been a simple act of abolition. At the same time, the Territory of Louisiana, by authority of Congress, took the name of Missouri; and, in 1819, the portion thereof which now constitutes the State of Arkansas was detached, and beame a Territory, under that name. In 1819, Missouri, which was then but thinly peopled, and had an inconsiderable number of slaves, applied for admission into the Union, and her application brought the question of extending the policy of the Ordinance of 1787 to that State, and to other new States in the region acquired from France, to a direct issue. The House of Representatives insisted on a prohibition against the further introduction of slavery in the State, as a condition of her admission. The Senate disagreed with the House in that demand. The non-slaveholding States sustained the House, and the slaveholding States sustained the Senate. The difference was radical, and tended towards revolution.

One party maintained that the condition demanded was constitutional, the other that it was unconstitutional. The public mind became intensely excited, and painful apprehensions of disunion and civil war began to prevail in the country.

In this crisis, a majority of both Houses agreed upon a plan for the adjustment of the controversy. By this plan, Maine, a non-slaveholding State, was to be admitted; Missoui was to be admitted without submitting to he condition before mentioned; and in all that art of the Territory acquired from France, vhich was north of the line of 36 deg. 30 min. f north latitude, slavery was to be forever rohibited. Louisiana, which was a part of hat Territory, had been admitted as a slave tate eight years before; and now, not only vas Missouri to be admitted as a slave State, ut Arkansas, which was south of that line, y strong implication, was also to be admitted s a slaveholding State. I need not indicate hat were the equivalents which the respective parties were to receive in this arrangement, irther than to say that the slaveholding States ractically were to receive slaveholding States, e free States to receive a desert, a solitude, in hich they might, if they could, plant the erms of future free States. This measure was lopted. It was a great national transaction— e first of a class of transactions which have nce come to be thoroughly defined and well nderstood, under the name of compromises. y own opinions concerning them are well iown, and are not in question here. According the general understanding, they are marked peculiar circumstances and features, viz:

First, there is a division of opinion upon me vital national question between the two ouses of Congress, which division is irreconable, except by mutual concessions of interts and opinions, which the Houses deem contutional and just.

Secondly, they are rendered necessary by pending calamities, to result from the failure legislation, and to be no otherwise averted in by such mutual concessions, or sacries.

Thirdly, such concessions are mutual and equal, or are accepted as such, and so become conditions of the mutual arrangement.

Fourthly, by this mutual exchange of conditions, the transaction takes on the nature and character of a contract, compact, or treaty, between the parties represented; and so, according to well-settled principles of morality and public law, the statute which embodies it is understood, by those who uphold this system of legislation, to be irrevocable and irrepealable, except by the mutual consent of both, or of all the parties concerned. Not, indeed, that it is absolutely irrepealable, but that it cannot be repealed without a violation of honor, justice, and good faith, which it is presumed will not be committed.

Such was the Compromise of 1820. Missouri came into the Union immediately as a slaveholding State, and Arkansas came in as a slaveholding State, sixteen years afterward. Nebraska, the part of the Territory reserved exclusively for free Territories and free States, has remained a wilderness ever since. And now it is proposed here to abrogate, not, indeed, the whole Compromise, but only that part of it which saved Nebraska as free territory, to be afterwards divided into non-slave holding States, which should be admitted into the Union. And this is proposed, notwithstanding an universal acquiescence in the Compromise, by both parties, for thirty years, and its confirmation, over and over again, by many acts of successive Congresses, and notwithstanding that the slaveholding States have peaceably enjoyed, ever since it was made, all their equivalents, while, owing to circumstances which will hereafter appear, the non-slaveholding States have not practically enjoyed those guarantied to them.

This is the question now before the Senate of the United States of America.

It is a question of transcendent importance. The proviso of 1820, to be abrogated in Nebraska, is the Ordinance of the Continental Congress of 1787, extended over a new part of the national domain, acquired under our present Constitution. It is rendered venerable by its antiquity, and sacred by the memory of that Congress, which, in surrendering its trust, after establishing the Ordinance, enjoined it upon posterity, always to remember that the cause of the United States was the cause of Human Nature. The question involves an issue of public faith, and national morality and honor. It will be a sad day for this Republic, when such a question shall be deemed unworthy of grave discussion and shall fail to excite intense interest. Even if it were certain that the inhibition of slavery in the region concerned was unnecessary, and if the question was thus reduced to a mere abstraction, yet even that abstraction would involve the testimony of the United States on the expediency, wisdom, morality, and justice, of the system of human bondage, with which this and other portions of the world have been so long afflicted; and it will be a melancholy day for the Republic and for mankind, when her decision on even such an abstraction shall command no respect, and inspire no hope into the hearts of the oppressed. But it is no such abstraction. It was no unnecessary dispute, no mere contest of blind passion, that brought that Compromise into being. Slavery and Freedom were active antagonists, then seeking for ascendency in this Union. Both Slavery and Freedom are more vigorous, active, and self-aggrandizing now, than they were then, or ever were before or since that period. The contest between them has been only protracted, not decided. It is a great feature in our national Hereafter. So the question of adhering to or abrogating this Compromise is no unmeaning issue, and no contest of mere blind passion now.

To adhere, is to secure the occupation by freemen, with free labor, of a region in the very centre of the continent, capable of sustaining, and in that event destined, though it may be only after a far-distant period, to sustain ten, twenty, thirty, forty millions of people and their successive generations forever!

To abrogate, is to resign all that vast region to chances which mortal vision cannot fully foresee; perhaps to the sovereignty of such stinted and short-lived communities as those of which Mexico and South America and the West India Islands present us with examples; perhaps to convert that region into the scene of long and desolating conflicts between not merely races, but castes, to end, like a similar conflict in Egypt, in a convulsive exodus of the oppressed people, despoiling their superiors; perhaps, like one not dissimilar in Spain, in the forcible expulsion of the inferior race, exhausting the State by the sudden and complete suppression of a great resource of national wealth and labor; perhaps in the disastrous expulsion, even of the superior race itself, by a people too suddenly raised from slavery to liberty, as in St. Domingo. To adhere, is to secure forever the presence here, after some lapse of time, of two, four, ten, twenty, or more Senators, and of Representatives in larger proportions, to uphold the policy and interests of the non-slaveholding States, and balance that ever-increasing representation of slaveholding States, which past experience, and the decay of the Spanish American States, admonish us has only just begun; to save what the non-slaveholding States have in mints, navy yards, the military academy and fortifications, to balance against the capital and federal institutions in the slaveholding States; to save against any danger from adverse or hostile policy, the culture, the manufactures, and the commerce, as well as the just influence and weight of the national principles and sentiments of the slaveholding States. To adhere, is to save, to the non-slaveholding States, as well as to the slaveholding States, always, and in every event, a right of way and free communication across the continent, to and with the States on the Pacific coasts, and with the rising States on the islands in the South Sea, and with all the eastern nations on the vast continent of Asia.

To abrogate, on the contrary, is to commit all these precious interests to the chances and hazards of embarrassment and injury by legislation, under the influence of social, political, and commercial jealousy and rivalry; and in the event of the secession of the slaveholding States, which is so often threatened in their name, but I thank God without their authority, to give to a servile population a La Vendee at the very sources of the Mississippi, and in the very recesses of the Rocky Mountains.

Nor is this last a contingency against which a statesman, when engaged in giving a Constitution for such a Territory, so situated, must veil his eyes. It is a statesman's province and duty to look before as well as after. I know, indeed, the present loyalty of the American People, North and South, and East and West. I know that it is a sentiment stronger than any sectional interest or ambition, and stronger than even the love of equality in the non-slaveholding States; and stronger, I doubt not, than the love of slavery in the slaveholding States. But I do not know, and no mortal sagacity does know, the seductions of interest and ambition, and the influences of passion, which are yet to be matured in every region. I know this, however: that this Union is safe now, and that it will be safe so long as impartial political equality shall constitute the basis of society, as it has heretofore done, in even half of these States, and they shall thus maintain a just equilibrium against the slaveholding States. But I am well assured, also, on the other hand, that if ever the slaveholding States shall multiply themselves, and extend their sphere, so that they could, without association with the non-slaveholding States, constitute of themselves a commercial republic, from that day their rule, through the Executive, Judicial, and Legislative powers of this Government, will be such as will be hard for the non-slaveholding States to bear; and their pride and ambition, since they are congregations of men, and are moved by human passions, will consent to no Union in which they shall not so rule.

The slaveholding States already possess th mouths of the Mississippi, and their territor reaches far northward along its banks, on on side to the Ohio, and on the other even to th confluence of the Missouri. They stretch thei dominion now from the banks of the Delaware quite around bay, headland, and promontory to the Rio Grande. They will not stop, although they now think they may, on the summit of the Sierra Nevada; nay, their arme pioneers are already in Sonora, and their eye are already fixed, never to be taken off, on th island of Cuba, the Queen of the Antilles.] we of the non-slaveholding States surrender t them now the eastern slope of the Rocky Mountains, and the very sources of the Mississippi, what territory will be secure, what territory can be secured hereafter, for the creation and organization of free States, within our ocean-bound domain? What territories on this continent will remain unappropriated and unoccupied, for us to annex? What territories, even if we are able to buy or conquer them from Great Britain or Russia, will the slaveholding States suffer, much less aid, us to annex, to restore the equilibrium which by this unnecessary measure we shall have so unwisely, so hurriedly, so suicidally subverted?

Nor am I to be told that only a few slaves will enter into this vast region. One slaveholder in a new Territory, with access to the Executive ear at Washington, exercises more political influence than five hundred freemen. It is not necessary that all or a majority of the citizens of a State shall be slaveholders, to constitute a slaveholding State. Delaware has only 2,000 slaves, against 91,000 freemen; and yet Delaware is a slaveholding State. The proportion is not substantially different in Maryland and in Missouri; and yet they are slaveholding States. These, sir, are the stakes in this legislative game, in which I lament to see, that while the representatives of the slaveholding States are unanimously and earnestly playing to win, so many of the representatives of the non-slaveholding States are with even greater zeal and diligence playing to lose.

Mr. President, the Committee who have recommended these twin bills for the organization of the Territories of Nebraska and Kansas hold the affirmative in the argument upon their passage.

What is the case they present to the Senate and the country?

They have submitted a report; but that report, brought in before they had introduced or even conceived this bold and daring measure of abrogating the Missouri Compromise, directs all its arguments against it.

The Committee say, in their report:

"Such being the character of the controversy, in respect to the territory acquired from Mexico, a similar question has arisen in regard to the right to hold slaves in the proposed Territory of Nebraska, when the Indian laws shall be withdrawn, and the country thrown open to emigration and settlement. By the 8th section of 'an act to authorize the people of the Missouri Territory to form a Constitution and State Government, and for the admission of such State into the Union on an equal footing with the original States, and to prohibit Slavery in certain Territories,' approved March 6, 1820, it was provided: 'That in all that Territory ceded by France to the United States under the name of Louisiana, which lies north of thirty-six degrees and thirty minutes north latitude, not included within the limits of the State contemplated by this act, slavery and involuntary servitude, otherwise than in the punishment of crimes, whereof the parties shall have been duly convicted, shall be, and is hereby, forever prohibited: *Provided, always*, That any person escaping into the same, from whom labor or service is lawfully claimed in any State or Territory of the United States, such fugitive may be lawfully reclaimed, and conveyed to the person claiming his or her labor or service, as aforesaid.'

"Under this section, as in the case of the Mexican law in New Mexico and Utah, it is a disputed point whether slavery is prohibited in the Nebraska country by *valid* enactment. The decision of this question involves the constitutional power of Congress to pass laws prescribing and regulating the domestic institutions of the various Territories of the Union. In the opinion of those eminent statesmen who hold that Congress is invested with no rightful authority to legislate upon the subject of slavery in the Territories, the 8th section of the act preparatory to the admission of Missouri is null and void; while the prevailing sentment in large portions of the Union sustains the doctrine that the Constitution of the United States secures to every citizen an inalienable right to move into any of the Territories with his property, of whatever kind and description, and to hold and enjoy the same under the sanction of law. Your Committee do not feel themselves called upon to enter into the discussion of these controverted questions. They involve the same grave issues which produced the agitation, the sectional strife, and the fearful struggle of 1850. As Congress deemed it wise and prudent to refrain from deciding the matters in controversy then, either by affirming or repealing the Mexican laws, or by an act declaratory of the true intent of the Constitution, and the extent of the protection afforded by it to slave property in the Territories, so your Committee are not prepared now to recommend a departure from the course pursued on that memorable occasion, either by affirming or repealing the 8th section of the Missouri act, or by any act declaratory of the meaning of the Constitution in respect to the legal points in dispute."

This report gives us the deliberate judgment of the Committee on two important points. First, that the Compromise of 1850 did not, by its letter or by its spirit, repeal, or render necessary, or even propose, the abrogation of the Missouri Compromise; and, secondly, that the Missouri Compromise ought not now to be abrogated. And now, sir, what do we next hear from this Committee? First, two similar and kindred bills, actually abrogating the Missouri Compromise, which, in their report, they had told us ought not to be abrogated at all. Secondly, these bills declare on their face, in substance, that that Compromise was already abrogated by the spirit of that very Compromise of 1850, which, in their report they had just shown us, left the Compromise of 1820 absolutely unaffected and unimpaired. Thirdly, the Committee favor us, by their chairman, with an oral explanation, that the amended bills abrogating the Missouri Compromise are identical with their previous bill, which did not abrogate it, and are only made to differ in phraseology, to the end that the provisions contained in their previous, and now discarded, bill, shall be absolutely clear and certain.

I entertain great respect for the Committee itself, but I must take leave to say that the inconsistencies and self-contradictions contained in the papers it has given us, have destroyed all claims, on the part of those documents, to respect, here or elsewhere.

The recital of the effect of the Compromise of 1850 upon the Compromise of 1820, as finally revised, corrected, and amended, here in the ace of the Senate, means after all substantially what that recital meant as it stood before it was perfected, or else it means nothing tangible or worthy of consideration at all. What if the spirit, or even the letter, of the Compromise laws of 1850 did conflict with the Compromise of 1820? The Compromise of 1820 was, by its very nature, a Compromise irrepealable and unchangeable, without a violation of honor, justice, and good faith. The Compromise of 1850, if it impaired the previous Compromise to the extent of the loss to free labor of one acre of the Territory of Nebraska, was either absolutely void, or ought, in all subseqent legislation, to be deemed and held void.

What if the spirit or the letter of the Compromise was a violation of the Compromise of 1820? Then, inasmuch as the Compromise of 1820 was inviolable, the attempted violation of it shows that the so-called Compromise of 1850 was to that extent not a Compromise at all, but a factitious, spurious, and pretented Compromise. What if the letter or the spirit of the Compromise of 1850 did supersede or impair, or in any way, in any degree, conflict with the Compromise of 1820? Then that is a reason for abrogating, not the irrepealable and inviolable Compromise of 1820, but the spurious and pretended Compromise of 1850.

Mr. President, why is this reason for the proposed abrogation of the Compromise of 1820 assigned in these bills at all? It is unnecessary. The assignment of a reason adds nothing to the force or weight of the abrogation itself. Either the fact alleged as a reason is *true* or it is *not* true. If it be untrue, your asserting it here will not make it true. If it be true, it is apparent in the text of the law of 1850, without the aid of legislative exposition now. It is unusual. It is unparliamentary. The language of the lawgiver, whether the sovereign be Democratic, Republican, or Despotic, is always the same. It is mandatory, imperative. If the lawgiver explains at all in a statute the reason for it, the reason is that it is his pleasure—*sic volo, sic jubeo.* Look at the Compromise of 1820. Does it plead an excuse for its commands? Look at the Compromise of 1850, drawn by the master-hand of our American Chatham. Does that bespeak your favor by a quibbling or shuffling apology? Look at your own, now rejected, first Nebraska bill, which, by conclusive implication, saved the effect of the Missouri Compromise. Look at any other bill ever reported by the Committee on Territories. Look at any other bill now on your calendar. Examine all the laws on your statute books. Do you find any one bill or statute which ever came bowing, stooping, and wriggling into the Senate, pleading an excuse for its clear and explicit declaration of the sovereign and irresistible will of the American People? The departure from this habit in this solitary case betrays self-distrust, and an attempt on the part of the bill to divert the public attention, to raise complex and immaterial issues, to perplex and bewilder and confound the People by whom this transaction is to be reviewed. Look again at the vacillation betrayed in the frequent changes of the structure of this apology. At first the recital told us that the eighth section of the Compromise act of 1820 was superseded by the principles of the Compromise laws of 1850—as if any one had ever heard of a supersedeas of one local law by the mere *principles* of another local law, enacted for an altogether different region, thirty years afterwards. On another day we were told, by an amendment of the recital, that the Compromise of 1820 was not superseded by the Compromise of 1850 at all, but was only "inconsistent with" it—as if a local act which was irrepealable was now to be abrogated, because it was inconsistent with a subsequent enactment, which had no application whatever within the region to which the first enactment was confined. On a third day the meaning of the recital was further and finally elucidated by an amendment, which declared that the first irrepealable act protecting Nebraska from slavery was now declared "inoperative and void," because it was inconsistent with the present purposes of Congress not to legislate slavery into any Territory or State, nor to exclude it therefrom.

But take this apology in whatever form it may be expressed, and test its logic by a simple process.

The law of 1820 secured free institutions in the regions acquired from France in 1803, by the wise and prudent foresight of the Congress of the United States. The law of 1850, on the contrary, committed the choice between free and slave institutions in New Mexico and Utah—Territories acquired from Mexico nearly fifty years afterward—to the interested cupidity or the caprice of their earliest and accidental occupants. Free Institutions and Slave Institutions are equal, but the interested cupidity of the pioneer is a wiser arbiter, and his judgment a surer safeguard, than the collective wisdom of the American People and the most solemn and time-honored statute of the American Congress. Therefore, let the law of freedom in the territory acquired from France be now annulled and abrogated, and let the fortunes and fate of Freedom and Slavery, in the region acquired from France, be, henceforward and forever, determined by the votes of some seven hundred camp followers around Fort Leavenworth, and the still smaller number of trappers, Government schoolmasters, and mechanics, who attend the Indians in their seasons of rest from hunting in the passes of the Rocky Mountains. Sir, this syllogism may satisfy you and other Senators; but as for me, I must be content to adhere to the earlier system. *Stare super antiquas vias.*

There is yet another difficulty in this new theory. Let it be granted that, in order to carry out a new principle recently adopted in New Mexico, you can supplant a compromise in Nebraska, yet there is a maxim of public law which forbids you from supplanting that compromise, and establishing a new system *there*, until you first restore the parties in interest there to their *statu quo* before the compromise to be supplanted was established. First, then, remand Missouri and Arkansas back to the unsettled condition, in regard to slavery, which they held before the Compromise of 1820 was enacted, and then we will hear you talk of rescinding that Compromise. You cannot do this. You ought not to do it, if you could; and because you cannot and ought not to do it, you cannot, without violating law, justice, equity, and honor, abrogate the guarantee of freedom in Nebraska.

There is still another and not less serious difficulty. You call the Slavery laws of 1850 a compromise between the slaveholding and non-slaveholding States. For the purposes of this argument, let it be granted that they were such a compromise. It was nevertheless a compromise concerning slavery in the Territories acquired from Mexico, and by the letter of the compromise it extended no further. Can you now, by an act which is not a compromise between the same parties, but a mere ordinary law, extend the force and obligation of the principles of that Compromise of 1850 into regions not only excluded from it, but absolutely protected from your intervention there by a solemn Compromise of thirty years' duration, and invested with a sanctity scarcely inferior to that which hallows the Constitution itself?

Can the Compromise of 1850, by a mere ordinary act of legislation, be extended beyond the plain, known, fixed intent and understanding of the parties at the time that contract was made, and yet be binding on the parties to it, not merely legally, but in honor and conscience? Can you abrogate a compromise by passing any law of less dignity than a compromise? If so, of what value is any one or the whole of the Compromises? Thus you see that these bills violate both of the Compromises—not more that of 1820 than that of 1850.

Will you maintain in argument that it was understood by the parties interested throughout the country, or by either of them, or by any representative of either, in either House of Congress, that the principle then established should extend beyond the limits of the territories acquired from Mexico, into the territories acquired nearly fifty years before, from France, and then reposing under the guarantee of the Compromise of 1820? I know not how Senators may *vote*, but I do know what they will *say*. I appeal to the honorable Senator from Michigan, [Mr. CASS,] than whom none performed a more distinguished part in establishing the Compromise of 1850, whether he so intended or understood. I appeal to the honorable and distinguished Senator, the senior representative from Tennessee, [Mr. BELL,] who performed a distinguished part also. Did he so understand the Compromise of 1850? He is silent. I appeal to the gallant Senator from Illinois? [Mr. SHIELDS.] He, too, is silent. I now throw my gauntlet at the feet of every Senator now here, who was in the Senate in 1850, and challenge him to say that he then knew, or thought, or dreamed, that, by enacting the Compromise of 1850, he was directly or indirectly abrogating, or in any degree impairing, the Missouri Compromise? No one takes it up. I appeal to that very distinguished—nay, sir, that expression falls short of his eminence—that illustrious man, the Senator from Missouri, who led the opposition here to the Compromise of 1850. Did he understand that that Compromise in any way overreached or impaired the Compromise of 1820? Sir, that distinguished person, while opposing the combination of the several laws on the subject of California and the Territories, and Slavery, together, in one bill, so as to constitute a Compromise, nevertheless voted for each one of those bills, severally; and in that way, and that way only, they were passed. Had he known or understood that any one of them overreached and impaired the Missouri Compromise, we all know he would have perished before he would have given it his support.

Sir, if it was not irreverent, I would dare to call up the author of both of the Compromises in question, from his honored, though yet scarcely grass-covered grave, and challenge any advocate of this measure to confront that imperious shade, and say that, in making the Compromise of 1850, he intended or dreamed that he was subverting, or preparing the way for a subversion of, his greater work of 1820. Sir, if that eagle spirit is yet lingering here over the scene of his mortal labors, and watching over the welfare of the Republic he loved so well, his heart is now moved with more than human indignation against those who are perverting his last great public act from its legitimate uses, not merely to subvert the column, but to wrench from its very bed the base of the column that perpetuates his fame.

And that other proud and dominating Senator, who, sacrificing himself, gave the aid without which the Compromise of 1850 could not have been established—the Statesman of New England, and the Orator of America—who dare assert here, where his memory is yet fresh, though his unfettered spirit may be wandering in spheres far hence, that he intended to abrogate, or dreamed that, by virtue of or in consequence of that transaction, the Missouri Compromise would or could ever be abrogated? The portion of the Missouri Compromise you propose to abrogate is the Ordinance of 1787 extended to Nebraska. Hear what Daniel Webster said of that Ordinance itself, in 1830, in this very place, in reply to one who had undervalued it and its author:

"I spoke, sir, of the Ordinance of 1787, which prohibits slavery, in all future time, northwest of the Ohio, as a measure of great wisdom and forethought, and one which has been attended with highly beneficial and permanent consequences."

And now hear what he said here, when advocating the Compromise of 1850:

"I now say, sir, as the proposition upon which I stand this day, and upon the truth and firmness of which I intend to act until it is overthrown, that there is not at this moment in the United States, or any Territory of the United States, one single foot of land, the character of which, in regard to its being free territory or slave territory, is not fixed by some law, and some IRREPEALABLE law beyond the power of the action of this Government."

What *irrepealable* law, or what law of any kind, fixed the character of Nebraska as free or slave territory, except the Missouri Compromise act?

And now hear what Daniel Webster said when vindicating the Compromise of 1850, at Buffalo, in 1851:

"My opinion remains unchanged, that it was not within the original scope or design of the Constitution to admit new States out of foreign territory; and for one, whatever may be said at the Syracuse Convention or any other assemblage of insane persons, I never would consent, and never have consented, that there should be one foot of slave territory beyond what the old thirteen States had at the time of the formation of the Union! Never! Never!

"The man cannot show his face to me and say he can prove that I ever departed from that doctrine. He would sneak away, and slink away, or hire a mercenary press to cry out, What an apostate from Liberty Daniel Webster has become! But he knows himself to be a hypocrite and a falsifier."

That Compromise was forced upon the slaveholding States and upon the non-slaveholding States as a mutual exchange of equivalents. The equivalents were accurately defined, and carefully scrutinized and weighed by the respective parties, through a period of eight months. The equivalents offered to the non-slaveholding States were: 1st, the admission of California; 2d, the abolition of the public slave trade in the District of Columbia. These, and these only, were the boons offered to them, and the only sacrifices which the slaveholding States were required to make. The waiver of the Wilmot Proviso in the incorporation of New Mexico and Utah, and a new fugitive slave law, were the only boons proposed to the slaveholding States, and the only sacrifices exacted of the non-slaveholding States. No other questions between them were agitated, except those which were involved in the gain or loss of more or less of free territory or of slave territory in the determination of the boundary between Texas and New Mexico, by a line that was at last arbitrarily made, expressly saving, even in *those Territories,* to the respective parties, their respective shares of free soil and slave soil, according to the articles of annexation of the Republic of Texas. Again: There were alleged to be five open, bleeding wounds in the Federal system, and *no more,* which needed surgery, and to which the Compromise of 1850 was to be a cataplasm. We all know what they were: California without a Constitution; New Mexico in the grasp of military power; Utah neglected; the District of Columbia dishonored; and the rendition of fugitives denied. Nebraska was not even thought of in this catalogue of national ills. And now, sir, did the Nashville Convention of secessionists understand that, besides the enumerated boons offered to the slaveholding States, they were to have also the obliteration of the Missouri Compromise line of 1820? If they did, why did they reject and scorn and scout at the Compromise of 1850? Did the Legislatures and public assemblies of the non-slaveholding States, who made your table groan with their remonstrances, understand that Nebraska was an additional wound to be healed by the Compromise of 1850? If they did, why did they omit to remonstrate against the healing of that, too, as well as of the other five, by the cataplasm, the application of which they resisted so long?

Again: Had it been then known that the Missouri Compromise was to be abolished, directly or indirectly, by the Compromise of 1850, what Representative from a non-slaveholding State would, at that day, have voted for it? Not one. What Senator from a slaveholding State would not have voted for it? Not one. So entirely was it then unthought of that the new Compromise was to repeal the Missouri Compromise line of 36 deg. 30 min., in the region acquired from France, that one half of that long debate was spent on propositions made by Representatives from slaveholding States, to extend the line further on through the new territory we had acquired so recently from Mexico, until it should disappear in the waves of the Pacific Ocean, so as to secure actual toleration of slavery in all of this new territory that should be south of that line; and these propositions were resisted strenuously and successfully to the last by the Representatives of the non-slaveholding States, in order, if it were possible, to save the whole of those regions for the theatre of free labor.

I admit that these are only negative proofs, although they are pregnant with conviction. But here is one which is not only affirmative, but positive, and not more positive than conclusive:

In the fifth section of the Texas Boundary bill, one of the acts constituting the Compromise of 1850, are these words:

"*Provided,* That nothing herein contained shall be construed to impair or qualify anything contained in the third article of the second section of the joint resolution for annexing Texas to the United States, approved March 1, 1845, either as regards the number of States that may hereafter be formed out of the State of Texas, or otherwise."

What was that third article of the second

section of the joint resolution for annexing Texas? Here it is:

"New States, of convenient size, not exceeding four in number, in addition to said State of Texas, having sufficient population, may hereafter, by the consent of said State, be formed out of the territory thereof, which shall be entitled to admission under the provisions of the Federal Constitution. And such States as may be formed out of that portion of said territory lying south of 36 deg. 30 min. north latitude, commonly known as the Missouri Compromise line, shall be admitted into the Union with or without Slavery, as the people of each State asking admission may desire And in such State or States as shall be formed out of said territory north of said Missouri Compromise line, slavery or involuntary servitude (except for crime) shall be prohibited."

This article saved the Compromise of 1820, in express terms, overcoming any implication of its abrogation, which might, by accident or otherwise, have crept into the Compromise of 1850; and any inferences to that effect, that might be drawn from any such circumstance as that of drawing the boundary line of Utah so as to trespass on the Territory of Nebraska, dwelt upon by the Senator from Illinois.

The proposition to abrogate the Missouri Compromise, being thus stripped of the pretence that it is only a reiteration or a reaffirmation of a similar abrogation in the Compromise of 1850, or a necessary consequence of that measure, stands before us now upon its own merits, whatever they may be.

But here the Senator from Illinois challenges the assailants of these bills, on the ground that they were all opponents of the Compromise of 1850, and even of that of 1820. Sir, it is not my purpose to answer in person to this challenge. The necessity, reasonableness, justice, and wisdom of those Compromises, are not in question here now. My own opinions on them were, at a proper time, fully made known. I abide the judgment of my country and mankind upon them. For the present, I meet the Committee who have brought this measure forward, on the field they themselves have chosen, and the controversy is reduced to two questions: 1st. Whether, by letter or spirit, the Compromise of 1820 abrogated or involved a future abrogation of the Compromise of 1820? 2d. Whether this abrogation can now be made consistently with honor, justice, and good faith? As to my right, or that of any other Senator, to enter these lists, the credentials filed in the Secretary's office settle that question. Mine bear a seal, as broad and as firmly fixed there as any other, by a people as wise, as free, and as great, as any one of all the thirty-one Republics represented here.

But I will take leave to say, that an argument merely *ad personam*, seldom amounts to anything, more than an argument *ad captandum*. A life of approval of compromises, and of devotion to them, only enhances the obligation faithfully to fulfil them. A life of disapprobation of the policy of compromises only renders one more earnest in exacting fulfilment of them, when good and cherished interests are secured by them.

Thus much for the report and the bills of the Committee, and for the positions of the parties in this debate. A measure so bold, so unlooked for, so startling, and yet so pregnant as this, should have some plea of necessity. Is there any such necessity? On the contrary, it is not necessary now, even if it be altogether wise, to establish Territorial Governments in Nebraska. Not less than eighteen tribes of Indians occupy that vast tract, fourteen of which, I am informed, have been removed there by our own act, and invested with a fee simple to enjoy a secure and perpetual home, safe from the intrusion and the annoyance, and even from the *presence* of the white man, and under the paternal care of the Government, and with the instruction of its teachers and mechanics, to acquire the arts of civilization and the habits of social life. I will not say that this was done to prevent that Territory, because denied to slavery, from being occupied by free white men, and cultivated with free white labor; but I will say, that this removal of the Indians there, under such guarantees, has had that effect. The Territory cannot be occupied now, any more than heretofore, by savages and white men, with or without slaves, together. Our experience and our Indian policy alike remove all dispute from this point. Either these preserved ranges must still remain to the Indians hereafter, or the Indians, whatever temporary resistance against removal they may make, must retire.

Where shall they go? Will you bring them back again across the Mississippi? There is no room for Indians here. Will you send them northward, beyond your Territory of Nebraska, towards the British border? That is already occupied by Indians; there is no room there. Will you turn them loose upon Texas and New Mexico? There is no room there.

Will you drive them over the Rocky mountains? They will meet a tide of immigration there flowing into California from Europe and from Asia. Whither, then, shall they, the dispossessed, unpitied heirs of this vast continent, go? The answer is, *nowhere*. If they remain in Nebraska, of what use are your Charters? Of what harm is the Missouri Compromise in Nebraska, in that case? Whom doth it oppress? No one.

Who, indeed, demands territorial organization in Nebraska at all? The Indians? No. It is to them the consummation of a long-apprehended doom. Practically, no one demands it. I am told that the whole white population, scattered here and there throughout these broad regions, exceeding in extent the whole of the inhabited part of the United States at the time of the Revolution, is less than fifteen hundred, and that these are chiefly trappers, missionaries, and a few mechanics and agents employed by the Government, in connection with the administration of Indian affairs, and other persons temporarily drawn around the post of Fort Leavenworth. It is clear, then, that this abrogation of the Missouri Compromise is not necessary for the purpose of establishing Territorial Governments in Nebraska, but that, on the contrary, these bills, establishing such Governments, are only a vehicle for carrying, or a pretext for carrying, that act of abrogation.

It is alleged, that the non-slaveholding States have forfeited their rights in Nebraska, under the Missouri Compromise, by first breaking that Compromise themselves. The argument is, that the Missouri Compromise line of 36 deg. 30 min., in the region acquired from France, although confined to that region which was our westernmost possession, was, nevertheless, understood as intended to be prospectively applied also to the territory reaching thence westward to the Pacific Ocean, which we should afterwards acquire from Mexico; and that when afterwards, having acquired these Territories, including California, New Mexico, and Utah, we were engaged in 1848 in extending Governments over them, the free States refused to extend that line, on a proposition to that effect made by the honorable Senator from Illinois.

It need only be stated, in refutation of this argument, that the Missouri Compromise law, like any other statute, was limited by the extent of the subject of which it treated. This subject was the Territory of Louisiana, acquired from France, whether the same were more or less, then in our lawful and peaceful possession. The length of the line of 36 deg. 30 min, established by the Missouri Compromise, was the distance between the parallels of longitude which were the borders of that possession. Young America—I mean aggrandizing, conquering America—had not yet been born; nor was the statesman then in being, who dreamed that, within thirty years afterwards, we should have pushed our adventurous way, not only across the Rocky Mountains, but also across the Snowy Mountains. Nor did any one then imagine, that even if we should have done so within the period I have named, we were then prospectively carving up and dividing, not only the mountain passes, but the Mexican Empire on the Pacific coast, between Freedom and Slavery. If such a proposition had been made then, and persisted in, we know enough of the temper of 1820 to know this, viz: that Missouri and Arkansas would have stood outside of the Union until even this portentous day.

The time, for aught I know, may not be thirty years distant, when the convulsions of the Celestial Empire and the decline of British sway in India shall have opened our way into the regions beyond the Pacific Ocean. I desire to know now and be fully certified of the geographical extent of the laws we are now passing, so that there may be no such mistake hereafter as that now complained of here. We are now confiding to Territorial Legislatures the power to legislate on slavery. Are the Territories of Nebraska and Kansas alone within the purview of these acts? Or do they reach to the Pacific coast, and embrace also Oregon and Washington? Do they stop there, or do they take in China and India and Affghanistan, even to the gigantic base of the Himalaya Mountains? Do they stop there, or, on the contrary, do they encircle the earth, and, meeting us again on the Atlantic coast, embrace the islands of Iceland and Greenland, and exhaust themselves on the barren coasts of Greenland and Labrador?

Sir, if the Missouri Compromise neither in its spirit nor by its letter extended the line of 36 deg. 30 min. beyond the confines of Louisiana, or beyond the then confines of the United States, for the terms are equivalent, then it was no violation of the Missouri Compromise in 1848 to refuse to extend it to the subsequently acquired possessions of Texas, New Mexico, and California.

But suppose we did refuse to extend it; how did that refusal work a forfeiture of our vested rights under it? I desire to know that.

Again: If this forfeiture of Nebraska occurred in 1848, as the Senator charges, how does it happen that he not only failed in 1850, when the parties were in court here, adjusting their mutual claims, to demand judgment against the free States, but, on the contrary, even urged that the same old Missouri Compromise line, yet held valid and sacred, should be extended through to the Pacific Ocean?

I come now to the chief ground of the defence of this extraordinary measure, which is, that it abolishes a geographical line of division between the proper fields of free labor and slave labor, and refers the claim between them to the people of the Territories. Even if this great change of policy was actually wise and necessary, I have shown that it is not necessary to make it now, in regard to the Territory of Nebraska. If it would be just elsewhere, it would be unjust in regard to Nebraska, simply because, for ample and adequate equivalents, fully received, you have contracted in effect not to abolish that line there.

But why is this change of policy wise or necessary? It must be because either that the extension of slavery is no evil, or because you have not the power to prevent it at all, or because the maintenance of a geographical line is no longer practicable.

I know that the opinion is sometimes advanced, here and elsewhere, that the extension of slavery, abstractly considered, is not an evil; but our laws prohibiting the African slave trade are still standing on the statute book, and express the contrary judgment of the American Congress and of the American People. I pass on, therefore, from that point.

Sir, I do not like, more than others, a geographical line between Freedom and Slavery. But it is because I would have, if it were possible, all our territory free. Since that cannot be, a line of division is indispensable; and any line is a geographical line.

The honorable and very acute Senator from North Carolina [Mr. BADGER] has wooed us most persuasively to waive our objections to the new principle, as it is called, of non-intervention, by assuring us that the slaveholder can only use slave labor where the soils and climates favor the culture of tobacco, cotton, rice, and sugar. To which I reply: None of these find congenial soils or climates at the sources of the Mississippi, or in the valley of the Rocky Mountains. Why, then, does he want to remove the inhibition there?

But again: That Senator reproduces a pleasing fiction of the character of slavery from the Jewish history, and asks, Why not allow the *modern patriarchs* to go into new regions with their slaves, as their ancient prototypes did, to make them more comfortable and happy? And he tells us, at the same time, that this indulgence will not increase the number of slaves. I reply by asking, first, Whether slavery has gained or lost strength by the diffusion of it over a larger surface than it formerly covered? Will the Senator answer that? Secondly, I admire the simplicity of the patriarchal times. But they nevertheless exhibited some peculiar institutions quite incongruous with modern Republicanism, not to say Christianity, namely, that of a latitude of construction of the marriage contract, which has been carried by one class of so-called patriarchs into Utah. Certainly, no one would desire to extend that peculiar institution into Nebraska. Thirdly, slaveholders have also a peculiar institution, which makes them *political* patriarchs. They reckon five of their slaves as equal to three freemen in forming the basis of Federal representation. If these patriarchs insist upon carrying their institution into new regions, north of 36 deg. 30 min., I respectfully submit, that they ought to reassume the modesty of their Jewish predecessors, and relinquish this political feature of the system they thus seek to extend. Will they do that?

Some Senators have revived the argument that the Missouri Compromise was unconstitutional. But it is one of the peculiarities of compromises, that constitutional objections, like all others, are buried under them by those who make and ratify them, for the obvious reason that the parties at once waive them, and receive equivalents. Certainly, the slaveholding States, which waived their constitutional objections against the Compromise of 1820, and accepted equivalents therefor, cannot be allowed to revive and offer them now as a reason for refusing to the non-slaveholding States their rights under that Compromise, without first restoring the equivalents which they received on condition of surrendering their constitutional objections.

For argument's sake, however, let this reply be waived, and let us look at this constitutional objection. You say that the exclusion of slavery by the Missouri Compromise reaches through and beyond the existence of the region organized as a Territory, and prohibits slavery FOREVER, even in the States to be organized out of such Territory, while, on the contrary, the States, when admitted, will be sovereign, and must have exclusive jurisdiction over slavery for themselves. Let this, too, be granted. But Congress, according to the Constitution, "may admit new States." If Congress may admit, then Congress may also refuse to admit—that is to say, may reject new States. The greater includes the less; therefore, Congress may admit, on condition that the States shall exclude slavery. If such a condition should be accepted, would it not be binding?

It is by no means necessary, on this occasion, to follow the argument further to the question, whether such a condition is in conflict with the constitutional provision, that the new States received shall be admitted on an equal footing with the original States, because, in this case, and at present, the question relates not to the admission of a *State*, but to the organization of a Territory, and the exclusion of slavery within the Territory while its *status* as a Territory shall continue, and no further. Congress has power to exclude slavery in Territories, if they have any power to create, control, or govern Territories at all, for this simple reason: that find the authority of Congress over the Territories wherever you may, there you find no exception from that general authority in favor of slavery. If Congress has no authority over slavery in the Territories, it has none in the District of Columbia. If, then, you abolish a law of Freedom in Nebraska, in order to establish a new policy of abnegation, then true consistency requires that you shall also abolish the Slavery laws in the District of Columbia, and submit the question of the toleration of slavery within the District to its inhabitants.

If you reply, that the District of Columbia has no local or Territorial Legislature, then I rejoin, so also has not Nebraska, and so also has not Kansas. You are calling a Territorial Legislature into existence in Nebraska, and another in Kansas, to assume the jurisdiction on the subject of slavery, which you renounce. Then consistency demands that you call into existence a Territorial Legislature in the District of Columbia, to assume the jurisdiction here, which you must also renounce. Will you do this? We shall see.

To come closer to the question: What is this principle of abnegating National authority, on the subject of slavery, in favor of the People? Do you abnegate all authority, whatever, in the Territories? Not at all; you abnegate only authority over slavery there. Do you abnegate even that? No; you do not and you cannot. In the very act of abnegating you legislate, and enact that the States to be hereafter organized shall come in whether slave or free, as their inhabitants shall choose. Is not this legislating not only on the subject of slavery in the Territories, but on the subject of slavery even in the future States? In the very act of abnegating, you call into being a Legislature which shall assume the authority which you are renouncing. You not only exercise authority in that act, but you exercise authority over slavery, when you confer on the Territorial Legislature the power to act upon that subject. More than this: In the very act of calling that Territorial Legislature into existence, you exercise authority in prescribing who may elect and who may be elected. You even reserve to yourselves a veto upon every act that they can pass as a legislative body, not only on all other subjects, but even on the subject of slavery itself. Nor can you relinquish that veto; for it is absurd to say that you can create an agent, and depute to him the legislative authority of the United States, which agent you cannot at your own pleasure remove, and whose acts you cannot at your own pleasure disavow and repudiate. The Territorial Legislature is your agent. Its acts are your own. Such is the principle that is to supplant the ancient policy—a principle full of absurdities and contradictions.

Again: You claim that this policy of abnegation is based upon a democratic principle. A democratic principle is a principle opposed to some other that is despotic or aristocratic. You claim and exercise the power to institute and maintain government in the Territories. Is this comprehensive power aristocratic or despotic? If it be not, how is the partial power aristocratic or despotic? You retain authority to appoint Governors, without whose consent no laws can be made on any subject, and Judges, without whose consideration no laws can be executed, and you retain the power to change them at pleasure. Are these powers, also, aristocratic or despotic? If they are not, then the exercise of legislative power by yourselves is not. If they are, then why not renounce them also? No, no. This is a far-fetched excuse. Democracy is a simple, uniform, logical system, not a system of arbitrary, contradictory, and conflicting principles!

But you must nevertheless renounce National authority over slavery in the Territories, while you retain all other powers. What is this but a mere evasion of solemn responsibilities? The general authority of Congress over the Territories is one wisely confided to the National Legislature, to save young and growing communities from the dangers which beset them in their state of pupilage, and to prevent them from adopting any policy that shall be at war with their own lasting interests, or with the general welfare of the whole Republic. The authority over the subject of slavery is that which ought to be renounced last of all, in favor of Territorial Legislatures, because, from the very circumstances of the Territories, those Legislatures are likely to yield too readily to ephemeral influences, and interested offers of favor and patronage. They see neither the great Future of the Territories, nor the comprehensive and ultimate interests of the whole Republic, as clearly as you see them, or ought to see them.

I have heard sectional excuses given for supporting this measure. I have heard Senators from the slaveholding States say that they ought not to be expected to stand by the non-slaveholding States, when they refuse to stand by themselves; that they ought not to be expected to refuse the boon offered to the slaveholding States, since it is offered by the non-slaveholding States themselves. I not only confess the plausibility of these excuses, but I feel the justice of the reproach which they imply against the non-slaveholding States, as far as the assumption is true. Nevertheless, Senators from the slaveholding States must consider well whether that assumption is, in any considerable degree, founded in fact. If one or more Senators from the North decline to stand by the non-slaveholding States, or offer a boon in their name, others from that region do, nevertheless, stand firmly on their rights, and protest against the giving or the acceptance of the boon. It has been said that the North does not speak out, so as to enable you to decide between the conflicting voices of her Representatives. Are you quite sure you have given her timely notice? Have you not, on the contrary, hurried this measure forward, to anticipate her awaking from the slumber of conscious security into which she has been lulled by your last Compromise? Have you not heard already the quick, sharp protest of the Legislature of the smallest of the non-slaveholding States, Rhode Island? Have you not already heard the deep-toned and earnest protest of the greatest of those States, New York? Have you not already heard remonstrances from the Metropolis, and from the rural districts? Do you doubt that this is only the rising of the agitation that you profess to believe is at rest forever? Do you forget that, in all such transactions as these, the people have a reserved right to review the acts of their Representatives, and a right to demand a reconsideration; that there is in our legislative practice a form of RE-ENACTMENT, as well as an act of *repeal;* and that there is in our political system provision not only for *abrogation*, but for RESTORATION also? And when the process of repeal has begun, how many and what laws will be open to repeal, equally with the Missouri Compromise? There will be this act, the fugitive slave laws, the articles of Texas annexation, the Territorial laws of New Mexico and Utah, the slavery laws in the District of Columbia.

Senators from the slaveholding States: You are politicians as well as statesmen. Let me remind you, therefore, that political movements in this country, as in all others, have their times of action and reaction. The pendulum moved up the side of freedom in 1840, and swung back again in 1844 on the side of slavery, traversed the dial in 1848, and touched even the mark of the Wilmot Proviso, and returned again in 1852, reaching even the height of the Baltimore Platform. Judge for yourselves whether it is yet ascending, and whether it will attain the height of the abrogation of the Missouri Compromise. That is the mark you are fixing for it. For myself, I may claim to know something of the North. I see in the changes of the times only the vibrations of the needle, trembling on its pivot. I know that in due time it will settle; and when it shall have settled it will point, as it must point forever, to the same constant polar star, that sheds down influences propitious to freedom as broadly as it pours forth its mellow but invigorating light.

Mr. President, I have nothing to do, here or elsewhere, with personal or party motives. But I come to consider the motive which is publicly assigned for this transaction. It is a desire to secure permanent peace and harmony on the subject of slavery, by removing all occasion for its future agitation in the Federal Legislature. Was there not peace already here? Was there not harmony as perfect as is ever possible in the country, when this measure was moved in the Senate a month ago? Were we not, and was not the whole nation, grappling with that one great, common, universal interest, the opening of a communication between our ocean frontiers, and were we not already reckoning upon the quick and busy subjugation of nature throughout the interior of the continent to the uses of man, and dwelling with almost rapturous enthusiasm on the prospective enlargement of our commerce in the East, and of our political sway throughout the world? And what have we now here but the oblivion of death covering the very memory of those great enterprises, and prospects, and hopes?

Senators from the non-slaveholding States: You want peace. Think well, I beseech you, before you yield the price now demanded, even for peace and rest from slavery agitation. France has got peace from Republican agitation by a similar sacrifice. So has Poland; so has Hungary; and so, at last, has Ireland. Is the peace which either of those nations enjoys worth the price it cost? Is peace, obtained at such cost, ever a lasting peace?

Senators from the slaveholding States: You, too, suppose that you are securing peace as well as victory in this transaction. I tell you now, as I told you in 1850, that it is an error, an unnecessary error, to suppose, that because you exclude slavery from these Halls to-day, that it will not revisit them to-morrow. You buried the Wilmot Proviso here then, and celebrated its obsequies with pomp and revelry. And here it is again to-day, stalking through these Halls, clad in complete steel as before. Even if those whom you denounce as factionists in the North would let it rest, you yourselves must evoke it from its grave. The reason is obvious. Say what you will, do what you will, here, the interests of the non-slaveholding States and of the slaveholding States remain just the same; and they will remain just the same, until you shall cease to cherish and defend slavery, or we shall cease to honor and love freedom! You will not cease to cherish slavery. Do you see any signs that we are becoming indifferent to freedom? On the contrary, that old, traditional, hereditary sentiment of the North is more profound and more universal now than it ever was before. The slavery agitation you deprecate so much is an eternal struggle between Conservatism and Progress, between Truth and Error, between Right and Wrong. You may sooner, by act of Congress, compel the sea to suppress its upheavings, and the round earth to extinguish its internal fires, than oblige the human mind to cease its inquirings, and the human heart to desist from its throbbings.

Suppose then, for a moment, that this agitation must go on hereafter as heretofore. Then, hereafter as heretofore, there will be need, on both sides, of moderation; and to secure moderation, there will be need of mediation. Hitherto you have secured moderation by means of compromises, by tendering which, the great Mediator, now no more, divided the people of the North. But then those in the North who did not sympathize with you in your complaints of aggression from that quarter, as well as those who did, agreed that if compromises should be effected, they would be chivalrously kept on your part. I cheerfully admit that they have been so kept until now. But hereafter, when having taken advantage, which in the North will be called fraudulent, of the last of those compromises, to become, as you will be called, the aggressors, by breaking the other, as will be alleged, in violation of plighted faith and honor, while the slavery agitation is rising higher than ever before, and while your ancient friends, and those whom you persist in regarding as your enemies, shall have been driven together by a common and universal sense of your injustice, what new mode of restoring peace and harmony will you then propose? What Statesman will there be in the South, then, who can bear the flag of truce? What Statesman in the North who can mediate the acceptance of your new proposals? I think it will not be the Senator from Illinois.

If, however, I err in all this, let us suppose that you succeed in suppressing political agitation of slavery in National affairs. Nevertheless, agitation of slavery must go on in some form; for all the world around you is engaged in it. It is, then, high time for you to consider where you may expect to meet it next. I much mistake if, in that case, you do not meet it there where we, who once were slaveholding States, as you now are, have met, and, happily for us, succumbed before it—namely, in the legislative halls, in the churches and schools, and at the fireside, within the States themselves. It is an angel of mercy with which sooner or later every slaveholding State must wrestle, and by which it must be overcome. Even if, by reason of this measure, it should the sooner come to that point, and although I am sure that you will not overcome freedom, but that freedom will overcome you, yet I do not look even then for disastrous or unhappy results. The institutions of our country are so framed, that the inevitable conflict of opinion on slavery, as on every other subject, cannot be otherwise than peaceful in its course and beneficent in its termination.

Nor shall I "bate one jot of heart or hope," in maintaining a just equilibrium of the non-slaveholding States, even if this ill-starred measure shall be adopted. The non-slaveholding States are teeming with an increase of freemen—educated, vigorous, enlightened, enterprising freemen—such freemen as neither England, nor Rome, nor even Athens, ever reared. Half a million of freemen from Europe annually augment that increase; and, ten years hence half a million, twenty years hence a million, of freemen from Asia will augment it still more. You may obstruct, and so turn the direction of those peaceful armies away from Nebraska. So long as you shall leave them room on hill or prairie, by river side or in the mountain fastnesses, they will dispose of themselves peacefully and lawfully in the places you shall have left open to them; and there they will erect new States upon free soil, to be forever maintained and defended by free arms, and aggrandized by free labor. American slavery, I know, has a large and ever-flowing spring, but it cannot pour forth its blackened tide in volumes like that I have described. If you are wise, these tides of freemen and of slaves will never meet, for they will not voluntarily commingle; but if, nevertheless, through your own erroneous policy, their repulsive currents must be directed against each other, so that they needs must meet, then it is easy to see, in that case, which of them will overcome the resistance of the other, and which of them, thus overpowered, will roll back to drown the source which sent it forth.

"Man proposes, and God disposes." You may legislate and abrogate and abnegate as you will; but there is a Superior Power that overrules all your actions, and all your refusals to act; and, I fondly hope and trust, overrules them to the advancement of the happiness, greatness, and glory of our country—that overrules, I know, not only all your actions, and all your refusals to act, but all human events, to the distant, but inevitable result of the equal and universal liberty of all men.

www.ingramcontent.com/pod-product-compliance
Lightning Source LLC
LaVergne TN
LVHW020639110826
845149LV00004B/1291

* 9 7 8 1 4 1 8 1 9 0 2 0 0 *